30 Wonderful Word Family Games

by Joan Novelli

SCHOLASTIC
PROFESSIONAL BOOKS

NEW YORK • TORONTO • LONDON • AUCKLAND • SYDNEY
MEXICO CITY • NEW DELHI • HONG KONG • BUENOS AIRES

Cover design by Norma Ortiz
Interior design by Solutions by Design, Inc.
Interior art by James Graham Hale except pages 45-48 by Kathy Couri
Poster artwork by Kathy Couri

ISBN: 0-439-20153-5

Copyright © 2002 by Joan Novelli.
Published by Scholastic Inc.
All rights reserved. Printed in the U.S.A.
7 8 9 10   40   09 07 06 05

Contents

About This Book

Jack and Jill went up the hill
to fetch a pail of water.
Jack fell down and broke his crown...

Nursery rhymes like this are easily picked up by many young children, who take great pride in being able to recite these tiny stories in their entirety. What nursery rhymes have in common, of course, is predictable text—in this case, words that rhyme. Children pick up on the repeated sounds of rhyming words and more easily remember them.

Rhyming words often (though not always) contain the same word family—a spelling pattern that stands for a sound. In "Jack and Jill," the words *Jill* and *hill* are part of the same word family (*-ill*), as are *down* and *crown* (diphthong /ou/). Teaching phonograms or word families as part of a reading program gives children tools for quickly and efficiently decoding many words—building success into early experiences with print.

This book is full of games you can use with your students to teach any word families. (A starter list of word families and words appears on pages 7 and 8.) Word families are by nature playful, making games the perfect approach for teaching them. By presenting this area of instruction in a playful way, you can reinforce the idea that learning to read can be full of fun. Some of the games, such as Ug, Ug, Bug! (see page 10), reinforce word families through twists on traditional games. Other games, such as Back to the Beehive (see page 23), come with reproducible activity sheets for reinforcing the skill. There are quiet games, such as Shake a Sound (see page 14), that children can play at their desks independently or with partners, and more active group games, such as Beach-Ball Word Builders (see page 9). The assortment of games makes it easy for you to vary the way students learn about word families, keeping their interest high as they strengthen reading skills.

Three Reasons to Teach With Word Families

 Children learn lots of words quickly.
Children with fairly good alphabet recognition skills can recognize consonants and the sounds they represent. These children can then easily learn a phonogram and apply the sound those letters make to read and spell new words. For example, a child who knows consonant sounds and the sound that the phonogram -*at* makes can read and write a good number of words, such as *bat, cat, sat, mat, hat, pat, rat,* and *flat.* Imagine the number of words a child can learn to read and write with just a few phonograms! That list grows quickly with every new phonogram taught.

 Word families can help children access more complicated phonics concepts.
Learning a phonogram sometimes makes more sense than learning the sounds that individual letters make. For example, in the word *car*, the letters *a* and *r* form the phonogram -*ar*. Knowing this, children can go on to recognize the words *far, jar, star*, and so on. This approach is more accessible to children than, for example, teaching *r*-controlled vowels.

 Word families lend themselves to playful learning experiences that stick with children.
Teaching with phonograms encourages playfulness with language. Rhyming words are fun to say and are predictable, making it easy for most children to latch onto the strategy and build reading fluency.

Phonograms and Rimes

A phonogram, the letters in a word family that stand for a sound, may also be referred to as a rime. The word *rime* is often used in conjunction with the word *onset*. Onset and rime refer to the two parts of a syllable. The onset is the consonant, consonant blend, or digraph that comes first. The rime is the vowel and everything that comes after. In the one-syllable word *truck*, the letters *tr* are the onset and the letters *uck* are the rime. In the two-syllable word *window*, there are two onsets (*w, d*) and two rimes (*in, ow*). Some words—for example, *at*—have no onset. (The letters *at* are the rime.)

Sample Word Family Lists
Sample word family lists appear on pages 7 and 8. These word families include phonograms from which the greatest number of primary-grade words can be generated. For a more complete list of word families, see *Phonics From A to Z*, by Wiley Blevins (Scholastic Professional Books, 1998).

 **Tip**

Teaching phonograms helps strengthen spelling skills, too. Phonograms have highly reliable spelling patterns. For example, children can confidently use the letters *a, c,* and *k* in that order to spell words, such as *Jack*, that have the -*ack* sound. The same idea applies to other phonograms children learn.

To Learn More

The Great Big Book of Fun Phonics Activities, by Claire Daniel, Deborah Eaton, and Carole Osterink (Scholastic Professional Books, 1999). Use this jumbo collection of easy activities, games, skill pages, and more to build early reading skills.

Mother Goose Phonics, by Deborah Schecter (Scholastic Professional Books, 1999). Activities, games, manipulatives, and learning center ideas for using favorite nursery rhymes to teach phonics skills.

Phonics From A to Z, by Wiley Blevins (Scholastic Professional Books, 1998). Pages 120 to 132 of this guide contain lists of phonograms, including short vowel, long vowel, variant vowel, and diphthong phonograms.

Phonics Games Kids Can't Resist, by Michelle K. Ramsey (Scholastic Professional Books, 1999). Easy-to-make-and-play games reinforce a range of phonics skills and are adaptable for both individual and group learning.

Phonics Make-and-Take Manipulatives, by Joan Novelli (Scholastic Professional Books, 1999). Reinforce word families and other phonics skills with reproducible mini-puzzles, word wheels, and more.

Word Family Wheels, by Liza Charlesworth (Scholastic Professional Books, 2000). These reproducible manipulative wheels help children master phonograms and strengthen reading skills.

Sample Word Family Lists
SHORT VOWELS

Short-*a* Phonograms

-ack   back, hack, Jack, lack, quack, rack, sack, tack, black, clack, crack, knack, shack, slack, smack, stack, track, whack

-an   ban, can, Dan, fan, man, pan, ran, tan, van, bran, clan, plan, scan, span, than

-ank   bank, Hank, rank, sank, thank, tank, blank, clank, crank, drank, Frank, plank, prank

-ap   cap, gap, lap, map, nap, rap, sap, tap, chap, clap, scrap, slap, snap, strap, trap, wrap

-ash   back, cash, dash, gash, hash, mash, rash, sash, clash, flash, smash, trash

-at   bat, cat, fat, gnat, hat, mat, pat, rat, sat, vat, brat, chat, flat, scat, slat, spat, that

Short-*e* phonograms

-ell   bell, cell, fell, jell, Nell, sell, tell, well, yell, shell, smell, spell, swell

-est   best, jest, nest, pest, rest, test, vest, west, zest, chest, crest, quest

Short-*o* Phonograms

-ock   dock, knock, lock, rock, sock, block, clock, crock, flock, shock, smock, stock

-op   bop, cop, hop, mop, pop, top, chop, crop, drop, flop, plop, prop, shop, slop, stop

Short-*i* Phonograms

-ick   Dick, kick, lick, Nick, pick, quick, Rick, sick, tick, wick, brick, chick, click, flick, slick, stick, thick, trick, wick

-ill   ill, bill, dill, fill, gill, hill, Jill, kill, mill, pill, quill, sill, will, chill, drill, grill, skill, spill, still, thrill

-in   bin, fin, kin, pin, tin, win, chin, grin, shin, skin, spin, thin, twin

-ing   bing, ding, king, ping, ring, sing, wing, zing, bring, cling, fling, sling, spring, sting, string, swing, thing, wring

-ink   kink, link, mink, pink, rink, sink, wink, blink, clink, drink, shrink, slink, stink, think

-ip   dip, hip, lip, nip, rip, sip, tip, zip, blip, chip, clip, drip, flip, grip, ship, skip, slip, snip, strip, trip, whip

Short-*u* Phonograms

-uck   buck, duck, luck, muck, puck, suck, tuck, Chuck, cluck, pluck, stuck, struck, truck

-ug   bug, dug, hug, jug, lug, mug, pug, rug, tug, chug, drug, plug, shrug, slug, smug, snug

-ump   bump, dump, hump, jump, lump, pump, chump, clump, grump, plump, slump, stump, thump

-unk   bunk, dunk, junk, sunk, chunk, plunk, shrunk, skunk, slunk, spunk, stunk, trunk

Sample Word Family Lists

LONG VOWELS

Long-*a* Phonograms

-ail   bail, fail, Gail, hail, jai,l mail, pail, quail, rail, sail, tail, wail, flail, frail, snail, trail

-ake bake, cake, fake, Jake, lake, make, quake, rake, sake, take, wake, brake, flake, shake, snake, stake

-ale bale, Dale, gale, male, pale, sale, tale, scale, stale, whale

-ame came, fame, game, lame, name, same, tame, blame, flame, frame, shame

-ate date, fate, gate, hate, Kate, late, mate, rate, crate, grate, plate, skate, state

-ay   bay, day, gay, hay, jay, lay, may, pay, ray, say, way, clay, gray, play, spray, stay, stray, sway, tray

Long-*e* Phonograms

-eat eat, beat, feat, heat, meat, neat, peat, seat, bleat, cheat, cleat, pleat, treat, wheat

Long-*o* Phonograms

-oke joke, poke, woke, yoke, broke, choke, smoke, spoke, stroke

Long-*i* Phonograms

-ice dice, lice, mice, nice, rice, price, slice, splice, twice

-ide hide, ride, side, tide, wide, bride, glide, pride, slide, snide, stride

-ight fight, knight, light, might, night, right, sight, tight, bright, flight, fright, plight, slight

Variant Vowel Phonograms

-aw gnaw, jaw, law, paw, raw, saw, claw, draw, flaw, straw

-ir   fir, sir, stir, whir

Good-Morning Game

Start the day with a game that lets students take time to visit a bit while building awareness of word patterns.

1 Make sets of cards on which you've written words that contain phonograms you are teaching. Use cards in fun shapes, such as stars or flowers, to add appeal.

2 Place a card in each child's cubby before the start of school. As children arrive, have them check their cubbies for their cards. Have them tape the cards to their shirts (or you may string them from yarn to make necklaces before putting them in cubbies) and then mingle with their classmates, saying "Good Morning" as they look for classmates with matching word family cards.

Beach-Ball Word Builders

Bring out a beach ball for a game your students will want to play again and again!

1 Cut pieces of masking tape and place them on the stripes of a beach ball. Write a phonogram on each piece of tape—for example, /ig/, /at/, /ock/, /ack/, /unk/, /ip/, and /est/.

2 Gather children in a circle and toss the ball to one child. Have the child who catches the ball choose the phonogram on the stripe under one of his or her hands and say a word that contains that word family—for example, if the child's hand is on /unk/, he or she can say *skunk*.

3 That child then tosses the ball to another child, who repeats the procedure. Continue until everyone has had a turn.

You can easily vary this game to keep it fresh and fun. Reinforce a single phonogram by writing words from one word family on the tape. Have children read the words on the stripes under their hands and then toss the ball to the next player. Or play Hot Potato. Have children say the word or words as quickly as possible and then toss the ball to the next person. You may time students to see how quickly they can read the words and toss the ball around the entire circle.

Ug, Ug, Bug!

Put a twist on the favorite game of Duck, Duck, Goose to reinforce children's understanding of any word family you want to teach.

1 Start by gathering children in a circle. Introduce a word family, such as /ug/. Let children suggest words that rhyme with *ug*—for example, *bug, dug, jug,* and *rug.*

2 Explain that you are going to go around the circle and tap children gently on the head or shoulder as you say "Ug, ug, ug." When you tap a child and say a word with the /ug/ sound, that child gets up and chases you around the circle, in the manner of Duck, Duck, Goose, trying to tag you before you sit in that child's space.

3 Once children understand the game, play a round using the phonogram and word you used to introduce the game.

4 If you get to the child's space before he or she catches you, take that child's place in the circle. Then have that child go around the circle, tapping children and saying "Ug, ug, ug," finally saying a word in the /ug/ word family and then repeating the chase around the circle.

5 If the child catches you first, that child sits back down and you repeat the circle procedure.

6 Repeat the game, using the same phonogram or introducing a new one. Children will enjoy the movement aspect and will listen carefully as they wait for you (or a classmate) to say the word that lets the chase begin.

Whispering Words

Children strengthen listening skills as they tune in to similar sounds in this quiet game.

1 Write word family pairs on index cards, one word per card. Make sure there is a card for each child and that each child will have a match.

2 Have children sit at their desks or tables and put their heads down and hands out. Go around the room, placing a card in each child's hand. When everyone has a card, have children look at their words then hold them facedown so that nobody can see their words.

3 Ask children to stand up and move about the room, whispering their words and listening for a child who is whispering a word that rhymes.

4 When children find their word partners, have them sit together. Play until everyone finds a match. Let children share their words (whispering them, of course), then let others add additional rhyming words that contain that phonogram.

Rhyming Freeze

Children listen for different word families in this fun-filled movement game.

1 Gather children in an open area. Invite them to run around as you shout out words that belong to the same word family. When they hear a word that doesn't belong, they should "freeze." Children who don't freeze sit down.

2 Play until one child is left. This child can then take a turn calling out words. Continue, using a different word family each time.

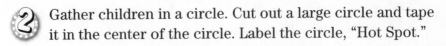

The Hot Spot

In this variation on musical chairs, players try to stay off the "hot spot" by listening to rhyming words.

1 To start, choose three phonograms to focus on. Write words that belong to these word families on index cards, one word per card. Shuffle the cards and give one to each child.

2 Gather children in a circle. Cut out a large circle and tape it in the center of the circle. Label the circle, "Hot Spot."

3 Stand in the center of the hot spot. Explain to students that you are the caller. You are going to say rhyming words, for example, *spot, hot, pot,* and *cot.* Children should listen to see whether the words you are saying rhyme with the word on their card. When they hear a word that doesn't belong in their word family—for example, *fish*—they step outside the circle and then go quickly around the circle to find and take an empty spot.

4 At the same time children are moving to a new spot on the circle, you should take one of their places. The child who does not get a space on the circle now goes to the hot spot and becomes the caller.

5 The new caller chooses one of the target words and starts calling out rhyming words, for example, *cat, hat, pat,* and *sat.* Again, when the caller says a word that doesn't rhyme, for example, *hop,* children who have words in the target word family step outside the circle and go around the circle to find an empty spot. (The caller also needs to quickly take a spot on the circle.) The player who ends up without a space goes to the hot spot and the game continues.

Follow the Footprints

Children strengthen word recognition skills as they hop from one end of a giant footprint path to the other.

1. Cut out a large foot shape. Use it to trace and cut out enough to stretch from one end of the room to the other.

2. Tape the footprints securely to the floor, spacing them to allow children to hop from one to another.

3. Write a word on each footprint. Include words from several word families. Alternate words so that the words from any one family are mixed in with words from the other word families.

4. Write additional words from the same word families on smaller footprint shapes. Place them in a basket or box.

5. To play, have children take turns selecting a word from the basket and then hopping on all the footprints that rhyme with that word.

Keep extra footprints handy. When you introduce a new phonogram, replace some of the footprints on the floor with fresh footprints (and new words).

Add-a-Word Beanbag Toss

Gather children in a circle for this fast-paced word family game.

1. Think of a word family you want to teach—for example, /ack/. While holding a beanbag (or some other soft object to toss), call out a word in that family, such as *quack*. Toss the beanbag to a child and have that child say another word in that family, such as *stack*.

2. Continue having children toss the beanbag to each other and say new words. Play until each child has had a turn. If you have more students than there are words, start a new game with a new phonogram. Encourage children to toss the beanbag to someone who hasn't had a turn.

Make a beanbag by filling a zipper-lock sandwich bag with dried beans. Close securely and toss!

Shake a Sound

Turn egg cartons into quick-and-easy game boards, to strengthen word recognition and spelling skills.

1. Start by writing a phonogram in each space of an empty cardboard egg carton. Prepare several egg cartons with different groups of phonograms, and let children play with partners.

2. Give each pair of children an egg carton, a penny, and a sheet of paper and a pencil.

3. Have players take turns placing the penny in the egg carton, closing the lid, and shaking the container. The player then opens the lid, removes the penny from the space, and says a word that contains the letter cluster shown. For example, if the penny lands on /ock/, the child might say *clock*.

4. Have children record the words they make. Players can vary the game by guessing how many turns it will take to have the penny land at least once in every space. Or, after so many turns, players can sort their words by phonograms to see how many of each they have.

Roll It, Say It, Spell It

In this easy-to-make game, children use phonograms to build words.

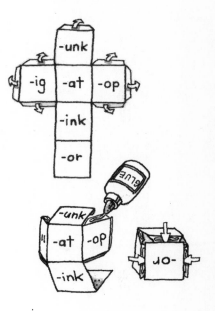

Tip

Let children take home their letter cubes. Invite families to play together, recording words they make. Have children bring their lists to school to share. How many different words for each word family did they make?

1 Give each child a copy of the letter cube pattern on page 31. Guide students in following the directions (see right) to make the letter cubes.

2 Have children roll their cubes, say the sound, then add a letter or letters to make a word. For example, if a child rolls an /ig/, she might say *big*. If a child rolls an /at/, he might say *bat*.

3 Copy the blank cube template on page 32 to make new word-building cubes. Write a different phonogram on each side of the cube. Copy for students to assemble.

Guess the Missing Letters

This game challenges children to find one phonogram that will complete all the words in a set.

1 Give children the following word frames:
   b __ __   f l __ __   t __ __   w __ __

2 Ask: "What two letters can you add to each of the words here to complete them?" (Remind students that the same letters have to work for each word.) Invite students to share their answers and tell the words they made. (One answer is *-ag*.)

3 Let children make their own versions of the game to share with classmates. Review them first to make sure they work, then compile them and make copies for students to try.

Tip

To simplify the game, write several phonogram choices on the chalkboard. Children can find the right one to fill in the words.

Roll-a-Rhyme

A ball is all you need for this simple rhyming game.

1 Have children sit in a circle. Roll a ball to one child, saying a word that contains a phonogram you want to reinforce.

2 Have the child who gets the ball say a word in the same family and then roll the ball to another classmate. That child says a new word that contains the same phonogram and rolls the ball to a new child.

3 The game continues until you've exhausted words with that phonogram or everyone has had a turn.

4 Start again with a new word family. Try playing with word families that correspond to children's names in the class—for example, *Jill*.

Fishing for Words

Stock a "pond" with "fish" and let children go fishing for words!

1 To make the pond, use a small wading pool. Or decorate a big cardboard box with blue paper.

2 Make multiple copies of the fish on page 33. Write a word from target word families on each fish. Then have children color in the fish and cut them out.

3 Attach a paper clip to each fish and place it in the pond. Make a fishing pole by tying string to a dowel. Tie a magnet to the end of the string.

4 Let children use the fishing pole to catch fish, touching the magnet at the end of the string to the paper clip on a fish.

5 Post chart paper next to the pond. Let children record the words they "catch" (grouping them by word families) and then add other words with the same phonogram.

Go Dish, Swish, Fish!

This version of the card game Go Fish lets children make matches by collecting rhyming words.

 Make multiple copies of the cards on page 33. Write one word on each card, making sure that each card has two word family matches. (See sample rhyming word pairs, below.) Let children play in groups of two to four.

 Guide children in following these steps to play.

❋ Deal seven cards to each player. Place remaining cards facedown in the middle.

❋ Have children take turns asking another player for a card by saying "Do you have a card that rhymes with [word]?" If the child asked has the card, he or she gives it to the other child, who then places the matching cards faceup on the table and reads them aloud.

❋ Another player with a card that matches this word family may add his or her card to the set.

❋ If the child does not have the card in question, he or she says "Go Fish" and the player selects a card from the deck.

❋ Play continues until children match all of their cards.

Make extra sets of the game cards and place them in zipper-lock sandwich bags. Let children take turns taking the games home to play with their families.

Go Fish Word List
Sample rhyming word pairs for Go Fish follow:

Long-*a*: cake, lake; face, race

Long-*e*: bee, tree; feet, meet

Long-*i*: bike, hike; mice, nice

Long-*o*: rose, nose; no, go

Short-*a*: bat, cat; cap, nap

Short-*e*: jet, pet; bell, tell

Short-*i*: pig, big; fish, dish

Short-*o*: hop, pop; rock, sock

Short-*u*: cup, pup; sun, fun

Ring Around Words

This arcadelike game will help children reinforce spelling and reading skills.

Tip

To vary the game, play a cooperative version. Have children combine their points and calculate the total. Let them play again and try to beat the class score.

 Fill five to ten large plastic soda bottles with water and cap tightly. (Add a few drops of food coloring to each, if desired.) Tape a label on each bottle. On each label write a word that represents a phonogram you're teaching. Underline the phonogram. Assign each bottle a number of points and write that number beneath the word.

② Arrange the bottles in an open area, placing the bottle worth the most points farthest away from a line on which children will stand to play. Gather several large rubber rings for children to toss around the bottles. Copy the score sheet on page 34 for each student.

③ To play, have children follow these steps.

✢ Stand on the tape. Toss a ring around a bottle.

✢ If you ring a bottle, say a word that is part of the same word family. On your score sheet, record the word under "Ring Around. . . ." Write your new word under "My New Word." Write the number of points you got for that bottle under "Points."

✢ Toss the rest of your rings. Record your new words and points. Add up the total number of points. Play again. Can you beat your score?

"Did You Ever See?" Silly Sentences

Turn a favorite Raffi song into a game that will bring out the giggles in your classroom!

1. Sing the Raffi song "Down by the Bay" together. The song is available on the CD *Singable Songs for the Very Young* and in the book *Down by the Bay: Raffi Songs to Read* (Crown, 1999). Keep the rhyming fun going by using the repeating pattern in the song to play a rhyming game.

2. Share the following sentence starter with students: "Did you ever see a king sitting on a _____ ?" Ask students to complete the sentence with a word that rhymes with *king*—for example, *swing*.

3. Now try this sentence starter: "Did you ever see a bat _____?" Let children complete the sentence any way they like, as long as the last word rhymes with *bat*—for example, Did you ever see a *bat* wearing a *hat?*

4. Once your students are comfortable with the procedure, share a new sentence starter that ends in a word that is easily rhymed. Let a volunteer complete the sentence as before. This child can then suggest a new sentence starter and choose a child to complete it. Play until you run out of ideas or time!

Children will have fun thinking of their own silly sentence starters. But if you'd like to write some on chart paper just in case, suggestions follow.

- Did you ever see a dog...
- Did you ever see Jake (or Jill or Kim...)...
- Did you ever see a clam...
- Did you ever see a sock...
- Did you ever see a bug...

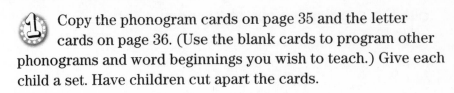

How Many in a Minute?

Children try to beat the clock when they play this word-building game.

1 Copy the phonogram cards on page 35 and the letter cards on page 36. (Use the blank cards to program other phonograms and word beginnings you wish to teach.) Give each child a set. Have children cut apart the cards.

2 Demonstrate how to form a word by placing a letter card and phonogram card together, as shown.

3 Tell children that you will time them for one minute while they build words with the letter and phonogram cards. They then build as many words as they can without reusing the letters.

4 When the minute is up, have children take turns reading aloud the words they made. Record them on chart paper, leaving out duplications. Count the words together. Play again and try to beat the class total.

Musical Words

This game will have children singing along as they learn about letter sounds and spellings.

1 Set up the game by writing on paper plates words that belong to target phonograms, one per plate. Make as many plates as there are children. On a slip of paper, write a word that belongs to each word family. Place these words in a bag.

2 Arrange the plates in a large circle and ask each child to stand by one (on the outside). Start the music and ask children to skip or walk around the circle. Stop the music and have children stand still in front of the nearest plate.

3 Pull a word out of the bag, then say it and show it. Have the child standing in front of the plate that has a matching phonogram read his or her word. Continue until each child has a chance to read a matching word.

Ringo!

Help children recognize word parts and patterns with Ringo!, a rhyming word version of Bingo.

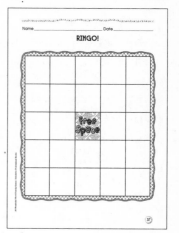

1 Make a class set of the blank Ringo! board on page 37. On the chalkboard, write 30 words that represent different word families. (See sample list below.)

2 Have children write one word in each square. They can write the words in any order, not necessarily the order in which they appear on the chalkboard. Tell students that they can use any of the words but that they will not use all of them. (This will result in each child having a different Ringo! board.)

3 For each word on the chalkboard, write a word on a slip of paper that belongs to the same word family. Place the papers in a bag.

4 To play, select one word at a time and read it aloud. Have children find a word on their boards that has the same phonogram. For example, if you say the word *hop*, a child might find the word *stop*. Have children place markers on squares that contain the same phonograms as the words you read.

5 Play until someone gets five across, down, or diagonally. Continue playing to allow more children to get "Ringo!"

Ringo! Word List

Use one word in each pair for the Ringo! board list. Write the remaining word on a slip of paper to be read aloud.

mash, dash	say, way	sink, pink
bug, tug	seat, neat	zip, lip
hop, stop	bell, tell	stir, whir
fan, ran	nest, rest	clock, rock
pack, stack	nice, rice	joke, poke
cake, lake	kick, stick	more, store
game, name	will, hill	dog, frog
tap, cap	fin, win	duck, luck
cat, bat	line, fine	bump, pump
gate, late	sing, wing	dunk, chunk

f	ish
b	ug
tr	uck
sk	unk
b	ack
p	ail
c	ake
f	an
b	ank
b	at
b	ell
b	est
n	ice
p	ick
h	ide
p	in
m	ine
r	ing
p	ink
cl	ock
j	oke
p	op
d	uck

To simplify the activity,
pass out letter squares
for one word at a time.
For example, give
three children the
letters *s u* and *n*. Ask
these children to
stand up and arrange
themselves to form a
word. Have a volunteer
read the word aloud,
and then let others
suggest words in the
same word family.

Move and Make Words

In this cooperative game, children match up to form new words.

1 On large squares of tagboard, write words that include phonograms you're teaching. For each word, write the onset (first letter or blend) on one square and the phonogram on a separate square. For example, write the letter *f* on one square and the letters *ish* on another to spell *fish*. Make sure that there is one square for each child. You may have more than one onset card with the same letter. (See samples, left.)

2 Pass out the squares, put on some music, and let children roam around the room looking for children they can team up with to build words.

3 When everyone has formed a word, let a volunteer from each pair read the word. (Depending on how children get together to form their words, some may end up without partners. This is a good time to have children work cooperatively, rearranging themselves so that everyone is part of a word.)

Back to the Beehive

In this word-building game, children help a bee find its hive.

1. Photocopy the game board and markers on pages 38 and 39. Tape the board together as indicated. Color and laminate, if desired.

2. Give each pair of children a game board and two markers. Have children cut and place one marker each on START.

3. To play, have children take turns tossing two pennies. If they both land heads-up, the player moves one space. If they both land tails-up, the player moves two spaces. If one lands heads-up and the other tails-up, the player moves three spaces.

4. After moving the correct number of spaces, the player says the sound represented by the phonogram on the space, then makes it into a word by adding a letter or blend to the beginning. For example, if a child lands on a space that says /ick/, he or she says the sound those letters make, then calls out a word in that family, such as *chick*. Let children play until both players reach the beehive.

How Many Words Can We Make?

Children team up to build words, words, and more words!

1. Write a phonogram on tagboard squares, one letter per square—for example, write the letter *u* on one square and the letter *n* on another. Write consonants and blends on additional squares.

2. Give the phonograms to children, one letter per child, and have them stand in front of the room. Give each remaining child a card with a consonant or blend on it.

3. Ask children to guess how many words they can make by combining their cards with the letters in front (the phonogram). Have children take turns going to the front to combine their letters with the phonogram. Record words they make.

4. Compare the total with the estimate. Did they make more words than they expected?

Rhyming-Word Relay Race

Children work in relay teams to generate rhyming words as fast as they can.

Rhyming-Word Relay Race

For each team, choose words that are equally easy to rhyme. Sample word sets (based on four teams) follow.

Set 1: cab, can, dad, bat

Set 2: jet, nest, fell, bed

Set 3: hid, pin, dip, sit

Set 4: cake, name, day, cave

1. Form groups of four to five students each for a relay race. Divide the chalkboard into as many sections as there are teams (or post chart paper for each team). Place masking tape on the floor where you want each team to line up.

2. Have students line up and close their eyes. Explain that you are going to write a word on the board for each team. When you say "Go!" they should open their eyes and, one at a time, go to the board and write a rhyming word under the team word. Team members may help one another with words and spelling.

3. Play until a set time is up (such as two minutes). Let a volunteer from each team read aloud the words. (See sample word sets, left.)

4. For more fun, give children additional relay race directions to incorporate as they go to and from the chalkboard—for example, "Hop on one foot to the chalkboard, write your word, then turn around three times before heading back to your team."

I'm Taking a Trip

Try this variation on an old favorite to reinforce phonogram sounds.

1. Gather children in a circle. Start by saying "I'm going on a trip and I'm taking a trunk."

2. Have the child to your left repeat your sentence and add a new word that has the same phonogram as your last word (*trunk*)—for example, "I'm going on a trip and I'm taking a *trunk* and a *skunk*."

3. The next child continues—for example, "I'm going on a trip and I'm taking a *trunk*, a *skunk*, and a *bunk*."

4. Play until children run out of words. Then suggest a new beginning and let children continue around the circle.

Find-the-Rhyme Basketball

Children practice "shooting hoops" and rhyming words with this engaging game.

① On slips of paper, write various words that represent phonograms you're teaching. Scatter them around a wastebasket.

② Use masking tape to mark two lines near the basket. Mark the line closest to the basket "1" and the line farthest away "3."

③ Tell students that you're going to say a word and one child will go up to the basket, find a word that rhymes, then crumple it up and shoot it into the basket from one of the lines. (The child chooses which line to shoot from.)

④ Record scores for each basket made (a 1 or a 3). Record the class score and save it. When you're ready to play again, discuss strategies for beating the class record.

Cleanup Spelling

This spelling game doubles as a cleanup activity!

1. Squirt shaving cream on each child's desk (or section of a table). Have children lather up their desks to get ready to play.

2. Say a word with a phonogram you want to reinforce. Ask children to use their fingers to write a word on their desks that belongs to the same word family.

3. Once everyone has a word, go around the room and let children share their words. Write them on the chalkboard, but do not repeat words. Count the words and record a total.

4. Have children "erase" their words to get ready to play again. Explain that you want to try to get even more words this time. What can children do to beat their first total? (*try to think of words nobody else will think of*) Say a new word and have each child write a word on their desks that belongs to the same word family.

5. Go around the room again, recording students' words. When it's time to wrap up, pass around a few clean rags and let children wipe their desks clean!

Silly Sentence Scramble

Children will giggle as they use words from the same word family to build silly sentences.

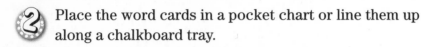 On sentence strips, write words that belong to a word family—for example, *Jake, snake, cake, bake, wake, shake, lake, rake,* and *take.* Trim to make word cards. Write additional words on sentence strips—for example, *of, the, an, and, a, so*—and trim. Cut sentence strips to make additional blank cards.

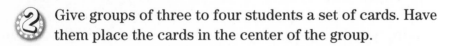 Place the word cards in a pocket chart or line them up along a chalkboard tray.

(3) Let children take turns arranging the cards one by one to build silly sentences. They can write other words they need on the blank cards. For example, in turn, children might arrange and add cards to make up this sentence: *Wake Jake to bake a fake snake cake and take it to the lake.*

Rhyming-Word Dominoes

This twist on the familiar game of dominoes helps reinforce words that belong to the same word family.

(1) Photocopy the domino cards on pages 40–42. Start by having children color the cards. Laminate first for durability, and then cut them apart.

(2) Give groups of three to four students a set of cards. Have them place the cards in the center of the group.

(3) Have the first player choose a domino and place it in the center of the playing area. Have the next player choose the next domino and try to connect it to the first by matching rhyming words. If the connection is made, the play continues to the next child. If no connection can be made, the child keeps the domino for another time and the next child takes a turn.

(4) Players continue connecting cards until no more matches can be made. They may use dominoes they were unable to connect on previous turns or select a new domino from the set.

Stock a center with copies of blank domino cards. (See page 40.) As students learn new word family spelling patterns, they can create new domino games to play.

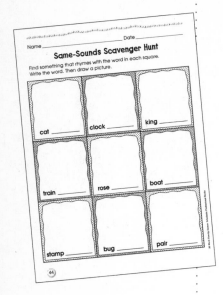

Same-Sounds Scavenger Hunt

Children pair up to search for things that have the same sounds as the words on game board squares.

1 Pair up students and give each team a copy of the game board on page 44. Start by reading the word in each square. Read the words again, this time having children read along with you.

2 Explain to students that they are going on a scavenger hunt for things around the room that rhyme with the words in the squares and have the same spelling pattern.

3 When they find something, they need to write the word and draw a picture. For example, for the word *cat*, children might find a classmate's hat, then write the word *hat* in the square and draw a picture of it. Let children share their findings with the class. How many different objects for each word did they discover?

4 To extend the activity, mask the words on the game board and make several copies of the blank board. Program each game board using different sets of words. Then copy, distribute to students, and play again.

Snaking Sounds

Play a movement game to reinforce long-*a* phonograms.

1 Start by saying the word *snake*. Ask children what sound the letter *a* makes in that word. Invite a child to say a word that rhymes with *snake*.

2 Have that child join hands with you as you begin to snake around the room. Stop by another child's desk and have him or her say another word with the /ake/ phonogram, such as *bake*. Have that child join the snaking chain as you move to the next child.

3 Continue until all children have joined hands to make one long snake. Snake around the room together, taking turns repeating the words.

Rhyming Red Rover

This twist on a classic outdoor game strengthens listening skills.

1. On index cards, write words representing several target phonograms. Write the word *It* on the other side. String with yarn to make necklaces. Give one to each child.

2. On a second set of cards, write a word that rhymes with each target phonogram (but is not on any of the necklaces).

3. Find a large space in which to play. Mark two lines at opposite ends of the space.

4. Give each child a word necklace. Invite a volunteer to be "It." Have this child turn his or her necklace so that the word *It* faces out. Give this child the second set of cards. Have everyone else wear the necklaces so that the other words face out.

5. Have the child who is "It" stand in the center of the space between the two lines. Have the other children stand behind one of the lines.

6. To begin, have that child call out, "Red Rover, Red Rover, let anyone whose word rhymes with [fill in word with target phonogram] come over!" Children wearing necklaces with words that rhyme must try to run to the line at the opposite end without being tagged by "It."

7. If the player is tagged, he or she turns the word card over so that it says "It" and joins the child in the middle. The game continues, with the original "It" calling another player: "Red Rover, Red Rover, let anyone whose word rhymes with [fill in word with target phonogram] come over!"

8. As more children are tagged, it will be increasingly difficult for players to get to the opposite end. When everyone has been called and is either safe or "It," let children trade necklaces and play again.

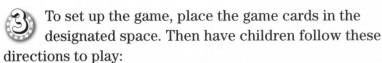

Teaching With the Poster: Read-Around-the-Town Rhyming Game

As children weave their way through the town on this game board, they'll use word families to make and learn new words.

Tip

This game is best played by small groups of children.

1 Laminate the game board for durability before showing children how to play.

2 Photocopy the game cards, spinner, and playing markers on pages 45–48 and cut them apart. Give each player a game marker to color. (You may also want to laminate these.) Then assemble the spinner and playing markers, as shown.

3 To set up the game, place the game cards in the designated space. Then have children follow these directions to play:

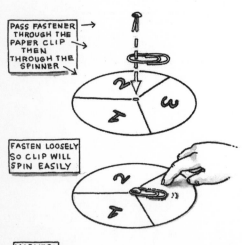

PASS FASTENER THROUGH THE PAPER CLIP THEN THROUGH THE SPINNER

FASTEN LOOSELY SO CLIP WILL SPIN EASILY

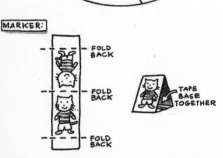

MARKER:

FOLD BACK
FOLD BACK
FOLD BACK

TAPE BASE TOGETHER

❧ Let children take turns spinning. Have them move the number of spaces indicated and then read and follow any directions on the square.

❧ Children can use the print that is part of the illustration on the game board for clues as they move and make new words. Encourage children to record words they make as they play.

❧ When all players have reached the last square (FINISH), let children read their words to you.

Word-Building Letter Cube

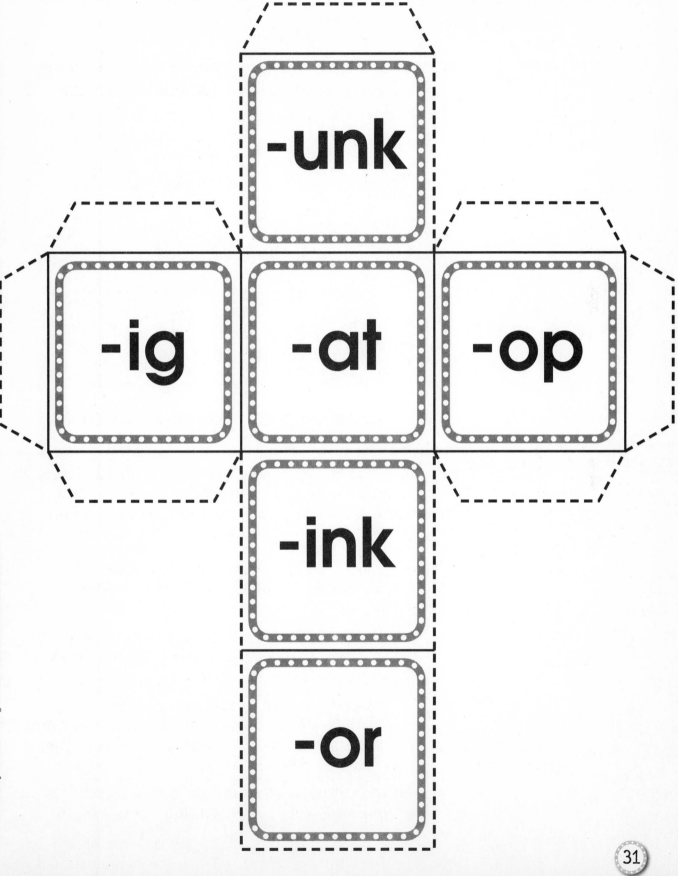

Word-Building Letter Cube Template

Note to the teacher: Use this blank template to make new word-building letter cubes. Make a copy of this page. Write a different phonogram on each side of the cube. Copy for students.

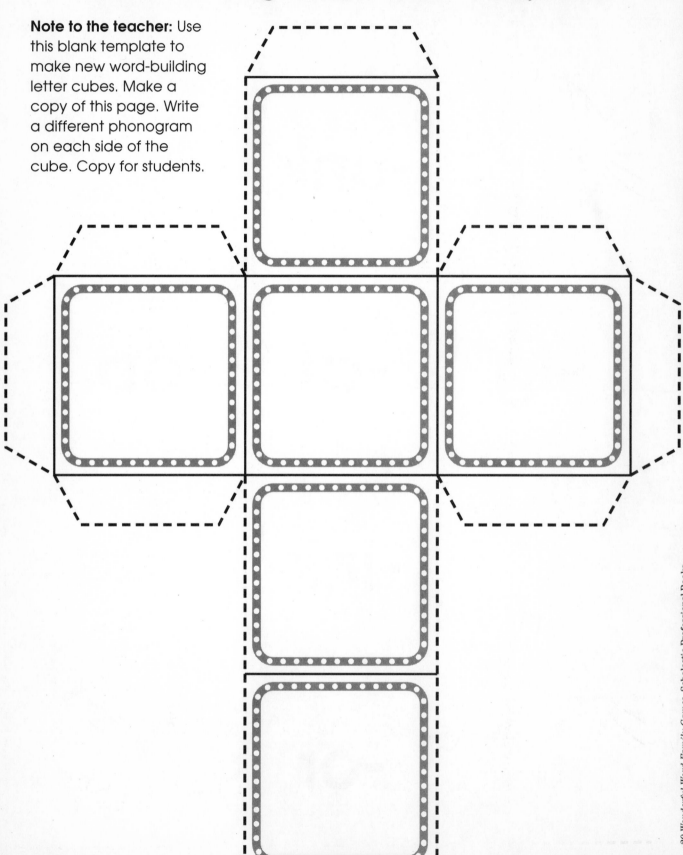

30 Wonderful Word Family Games Scholastic Professional Books

Fish Game Cards

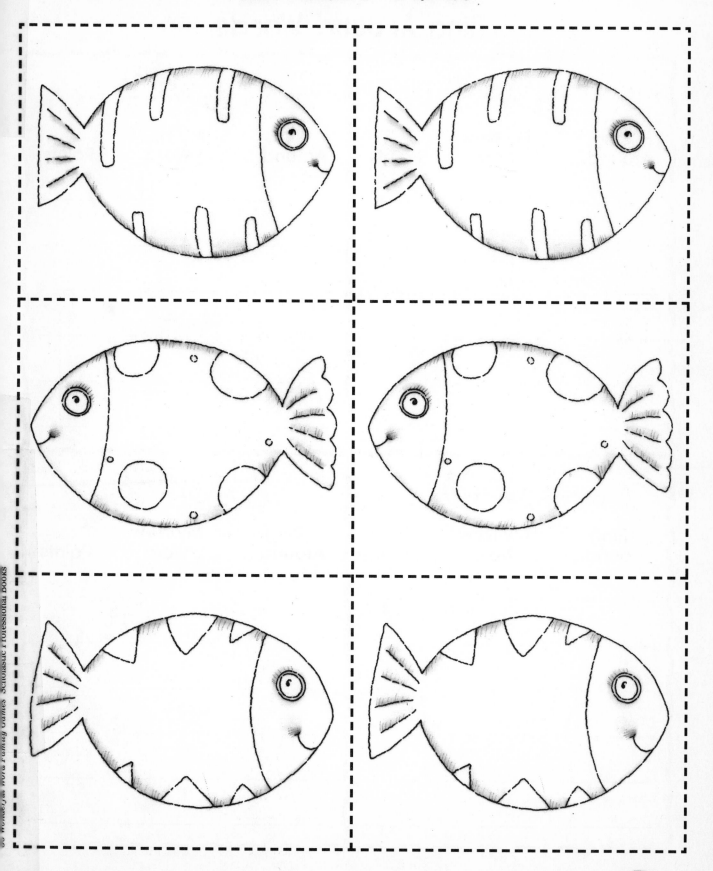

Ring Around Words

GAME 1

Ring Around...	My New Word	Points
_____	_____	_____
_____	_____	_____
_____	_____	_____
_____	_____	_____
_____	_____	_____
_____	_____	_____

GAME 2

Ring Around...	My New Word	Points
_____	_____	_____
_____	_____	_____
_____	_____	_____
_____	_____	_____
_____	_____	_____
_____	_____	_____

GAME 3

Ring Around...	My New Word	Points
_____	_____	_____
_____	_____	_____
_____	_____	_____
_____	_____	_____
_____	_____	_____

GAME 4

Ring Around...	My New Word	Points
_____	_____	_____
_____	_____	_____
_____	_____	_____
_____	_____	_____
_____	_____	_____

30 Wonderful Word Family Games Scholastic Professional Books

How Many in a Minute?

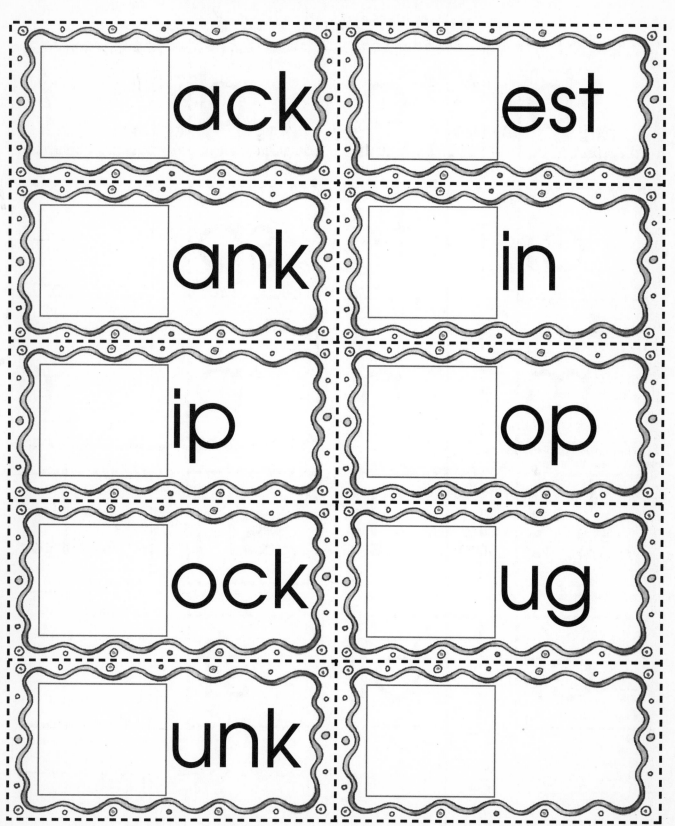

ack

est

ank

in

ip

op

ock

ug

unk

How Many in a Minute?

b	c	d	f
cl	tr	sp	l
m	n	p	r
s	t	sn	ch
cr	bl	st	

40 Wonderful Word Family Games Scholastic Professional Books

RINGO!

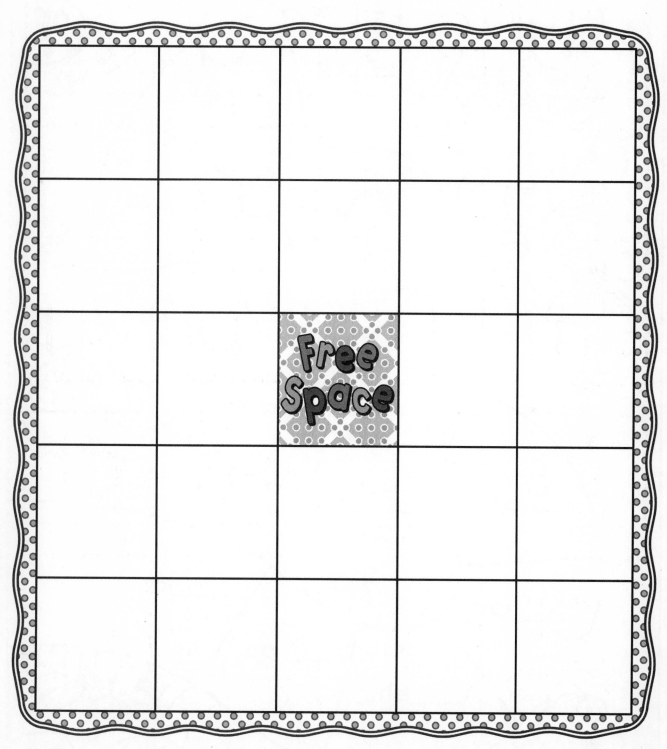

START

____og

____ig

____an

____ub

____ip

____old

____en

____ide

____it

____op

____ap

____ish

the Beehive

____ice

____ose

____ock

____ob

____ag

____ill

____est

FINISH

____oat

____un

____ink

____am   ____ot

Rhyming-Word Dominoes

cake	nail	pail	bee
tee	snake	boat	snail
rake	coat	knee	float
tail	snowflake	goat	mail
lake	three	throat	tree

Rhyming-Word Dominoes

swing	rock	can	bat

hat	pan	rat	king

fan	wing	block	man

sock	mat	ring	cat

string	clock	van	lock

30 Wonderful Word Family Games Scholastic Professional Books

Rhyming-Word Dominoes

bug	hill	stop	grill
shell	cop	yell	mug
mop	hug	bill	fell
ill	top	tug	drill
rug	bell	well	pop

30 Wonderful Word Family Games Scholastic Professional Books

Rhyming-Word Domino Templates

Same-Sounds Scavenger Hunt

Find something that rhymes with the word in each square.
Write the word. Then draw a picture.

cat _____	**clock** _____	**king** _____
train _____	**rose** _____	**boat** _____
stamp _____	**bug** _____	**pair** _____

30 Wonderful Word Family Games Scholastic Professional Books

Poster Game Cards

Make a word that
rhymes with *snack*.

_____ack

Go back
two spaces.

Go ahead
two spaces.

Trade places with
any other player.

Say a word
that rhymes with
found and *hound*.
Spell it!

Go back
one space.

Go ahead
one space.

Take another turn.

Poster Game Cards

Unscramble these letters
to make a word.
Say a word that rhymes.

t c a

Unscramble these letters
to make a word.
Say a word that rhymes.

p g i

Say the word below.
Change a letter to make
a rhyming word.

sun   __un

Tell a story.
Use the words
found, *hound*,
and *ground*.

Tell a story.
Use the words
Jake, *cake*, and *shake*.

Hop on one foot while
you say five words
that rhyme with *hop*.

Shake hands with the
player to your left.
Say four words that
rhyme with *shake*.

Quack like a duck.
Say two words that
rhyme with *quack*.

30 Wonderful Word Family Games Scholastic Professional Books

Poster Game Cards

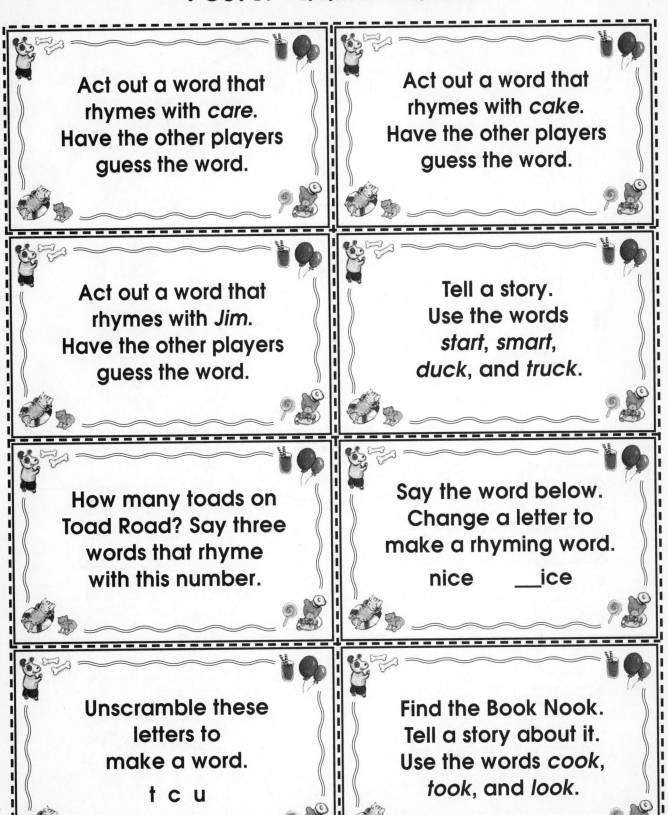

Act out a word that rhymes with *care*. Have the other players guess the word.

Act out a word that rhymes with *cake*. Have the other players guess the word.

Act out a word that rhymes with *Jim*. Have the other players guess the word.

Tell a story. Use the words *start*, *smart*, *duck*, and *truck*.

How many toads on Toad Road? Say three words that rhyme with this number.

Say the word below. Change a letter to make a rhyming word.

nice   __ice

Unscramble these letters to make a word.

t c u

Find the Book Nook. Tell a story about it. Use the words *cook*, *took*, and *look*.

Poster Game Spinner and Playing Markers

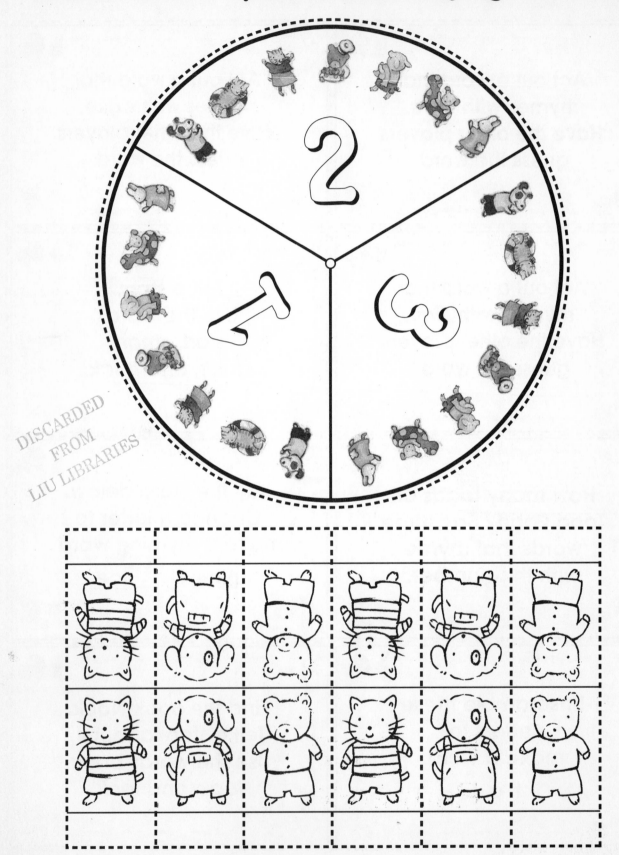